UNIVERSITY SUCCESS

Tips From A University Professor

Brian Harris, B.A., M.Ed.

ISBN 978-0-929079-51-6

CGS Communications, Inc.

HOW TO BE A SUCCESSFUL UNIVERSITY STUDENT

On average almost one out of every two students who starts any university around the world never completes his/her degree. This book is intended to help you to be one of the graduating students.

For more than 20 years I was the Department Head of Guidance in several Ontario high schools. I have also taught part-time at the University of Toronto, York University, and I am currently teaching at Queen's University. These experiences have given me firsthand knowledge to help me write this book to assist you to be more successful in university.

While my experience as a high school counsellor gave me some great insights into why students choose certain universities and programs, my experiences in working in universities gives me a strong understanding of what students have to do to be successful at university.

As previously stated, the intent of this book is to help you to be more successful at university, to help you to be one of the graduating students. It has been said that success leaves clues. In this book I will present some of the clues and some of the practical strategies and tips that I have seen students use to be more successful in university.

Rather than provide an essay style format to give my observations, I have chosen to present the tips and strategies in short one sentence bites of information. This format allows you to read a page or two at your own convenience. You can even pick up the book and start in the middle if you wish, or for the really creative, you can start at the end of the book and work backwards.

The manner in which you read this book is not as important as finding a few tips and strategies that you can actually use to help make a positive difference in your university studies. Every tip in this book is not intended for every student. It is up to you to explore and find some tips in this book that can help you to be more successful.

The tips in this book could be grouped (although they aren't) into 7 categories. The categories that contribute to being a successful university student are as follows:

i) Choose a program that builds on your strengths.

ii) Find a healthy balance between your social life and your academic studies.

iii) Success favours those who are prepared.

iv) Understand the difference between high school and university.

v) Know where to get help.

vi) Have a reason to succeed.

vii) Believe that you can succeed.

Before providing 401 tips to help you to be

more successful in university, I would like to provide a few thoughts on each of the 7 factors on the previous page. This can help you to better understand the tips that you will be looking at in the remainder of this book.

i) CHOOSE A PROGRAM THAT BUILDS ON YOUR STRENGTHS

One of the most important contributors to being successful in anything that you do is to build on your strengths. Marcus Buckingham, in his bestselling book *Go Put Your Strengths To Work* states, "A little less than two out of ten people succeed in capitalizing on their strengths. And as the research reveals, those two people are significantly more productive. Your strengths magnify you."

The most successful businesses build on their employee's strengths. For example, at Toyota all new managers must attend a three day Great Manager program that shows them how to spot the strengths of the people they supervise. At Yahoo, all new managers are required to take an online survey that measures their talents and pinpoints their strengths.

In working with high school students for over 20 years, I stressed the importance of choosing a university program that was based on their strengths. Your strengths are a combination of your interests and your abilities (and your values).

Let me provide a few examples of what I am talking about. Derrick was a university student who struggled during his first semester of studies. He was in a science program, largely due to his perception that this was an area that might help him get a good job when he graduated. Derrick was unsuccessful because his program was not based on his interests and his abilities. In high school, Derrick's real love was English and to be more precise, creative writing. In addition to this being Derrick's strongest interest in high school, it was also the subject where he achieved his highest marks.

In other words, English (and creative writing) was an area that was Derrick's strength because it was based on both his interests and abilities. It was also based on his values because he believed that writers could make an important contribution to our world. After a dismal first term in university, Derrick changed his program emphasis to English where he instantly enjoyed great success.

Confucius said, "Find a job that you love, and you will never have to work a day in your life." The same is true in university. Find a program that you love (and that you do well), and university will be much more pleasurable (and successful) for you.

Interestingly, most people think that the key to success is working on their weaknesses. In reality, the opposite is true. In a 2001 poll, only 41% of Americans chose building on their strengths as the key to success while in the UK and Canada, this percentage dropped to 38%, and in Japan and China, only 24% of the people surveyed believed that success came from building on their strengths. Success is related to what you believe. Success is best attained by building on your strengths, but if you believe that success is best attained by focussing on your weaknesses, you might expend a great amount of effort in your studies, but still be unsuccessful.

The truth is that you will be more successful in university (and in your future occupation) when you focus on what you love to do and what you do best.

Nicole enjoyed the study of languages; she also loved to play the piano. When she chose her university program, she decided to study languages. In spite of passing grades after first year, Nicole never returned back to university for her second year of studies. It looked like Nicole was going to be one of the two students who start university, but who never graduate. Success in university isn't always about ability. Nicole had the ability to be successful in languages at university but when asked why she decided not to return back to university after her first year of studies, she said, "My heart wasn't in what I was doing."

After taking a year off, Nicole then returned back to university to study music. This time, she was incredibly successful and very happy. Playing the piano was Nicole's love. This is what she did best, and this is what gave her great pleasure. Nicole eventually graduated from university, having a very successful experience, and she went on to have an equally successful career in the music industry.

Not only should your program be based on your strengths (your interests and abilities), but most of the courses you choose within your program should also be based on your strengths. Before you register for your classes at the beginning of a school year, it makes a lot of sense to look at all the courses that are available to you in your program of studies. Ask yourself: "Which courses do I have to take? Which courses are optional for me? Which courses will build on my abilities and interests?" Read the course descriptions and if possible, consult with other students who have taken the courses. You can also schedule an appointment within the Department of your main interests to talk to a Faculty member about your course selections.

When you build on your strengths you will be more optimistic about school. If you do encounter any obstacles you will be more resilient in facing them and overcoming them.

When you build on your strengths, you will feel better about yourself. You will be happier. You will be more confident. You will be more successful.

ii) FIND A HEALTHY BALANCE BETWEEN YOUR SOCIAL LIFE AND YOUR ACADEMIC STUDIES

There is no doubt that a significant number of students who are unsuccessful in university have spent too much time "having fun" and too little time in their actual studies.

As a high school counsellor I often invited

former graduates from our school who were now in university to return back to our high school to talk to our students about their experiences in university. When I first started doing this, I became aware that some students who were now in university enjoyed talking about the parties, the bars, and in general all the fun they were having. Other students talked more about their courses. After a few years of being involved in this activity, I decided to conduct an informal survey of how what a university student emphasized affected their actual success.

Although this was an informal study, based on approximately 125 students, here is what I found. Ninety-one percent of the students (now in university) who talked primarily about their courses and their learning in their first year of university successfully completed their first year of studies. On the other hand, only 43% of the students who focussed on talking about the parties and their great social life were successful at the end of their first year.

Of additional interest, of the 9% of the serious students who were not successful, in follow up interviews with several of these students, I discovered that many of them were doing very well up until their final exams when either stress or an illness sidelined them. It is possible that these students might have failed to have some non-academic activities in their life at university. While the main purpose of university is to learn, there is still a need to have some fun.

In my experience, students who quickly adapt to university life and enjoy their courses are those who get involved in some way at the university: whether it's through a club, a team, volunteer work, or some other form of campus activity. I often hear successful students talking about being a part of orientation activities that helped them to feel more comfortable on campus. Such activities often have the added bonus of helping students to make new friends.

I am sometimes asked if there is a recommended ratio between "studying" and "playing". In other words, what students are asking is something along the lines of "Should I spend 80% of my time focussing on my course requirements and 20% of my time doing something other than my course work?" I don't have an answer to this question, at least not an answer that provides specific percentages. What I would say though is that the greatest amount of your time should be spent focussing on attending your classes, completing your homework, preparing for your next day's classes, and preparing for future tests and assignment. Having said this, there is a need to spend at least an hour or two each day having fun with your friends and/or being involved in some form of recreational activity (even if it's just going for a walk; and better yet, going for a walk with a friend).

One of the most important aspects of achieving a balance in your life is getting enough sleep. Consider the following facts from the National Sleep Research Project in Australia:

- 17 hours of sustained wakefulness leads to a decrease in performance

- exposure to noise at night can suppress the immune function even if the sleeper doesn't wake up

- unfamiliar noise during the first two hours of sleep and the last two hours have the greatest disruption on the sleep cycle

- teenagers need as much sleep as small children (10 hours a night)

- as a group, 18-24 year olds who are deprived of sleep suffer more from impaired performance than older adults

Getting enough sleep can make a positive difference in helping you to be successful at university because it helps you to perform at your highest level and also helps to prevent you from getting sick.

Having said this, consider the above facts

from the National Sleep Project once again. If you are living away from home while you are attending university, it might be more difficult for you to adjust to your new surroundings and get a good night's sleep. In addition, due to possible noises around you, your sleep cycle might be affected leaving you feeling tired and resulting in performing at a lower level. Finally, if you regularly stay awake for more than 17 hours at a time (for whatever reason), this will lead to a decrease in performance. It is a common practice for some students to study well into the early morning before exams. The lack of sleep from such studying habits can lead to a decreased performance on your exams.

In addition to getting enough sleep, it is important each day to have some kind of physical release. This could include walking, swimming, jogging, riding a bike, yoga, and so on. The key factor here is that exercise helps to reduce stress. Allowing stress to build in your body over weeks and even months, paired together with poor sleep habits, will cause reduced performance which could have a detrimental affect on your assignments and exams (and your health).

Another important aspect of having a positive balance in your life is to eat (and drink) healthy. The first rule of good eating is to have a healthy nutritious breakfast. Unfortunately some university students tend to get up at the last minute and have nothing more than a coffee or soda for breakfast. This is not healthy, nor is snacking on junk food throughout the day. We all know these things, but for some students it's easier (and quicker) to eat foods that they know are unhealthy than it is to take the time to eat properly. Peak success requires attention to what you eat and drink.

Finally, in order to have a more positive balance in your life, you might have to learn to say no. With so many clubs and other activities at university, it is easy to get overinvolved. It might also be easy to promise a friend that you will do something for them. Saying yes to everyone else can leave you exhausted. You are attending university to increase your skills and knowledge. This can be difficult to accomplish if you are too tired to complete your assignments or study because you are spending too much time meeting the needs of others. Sometimes in order to achieve a balance in your life, you need to be selfish; you need to learn to say no.

Another significant aspect of finding balance in your life is to prioritize what you have to do. If you want to be one of the graduating students at your university (and I hope this is your goal), then you need to spend your greatest time and your best efforts in tasks directly related to successfully completing your courses. This means that attending all your classes should be a number one priority. Spending a specific amount of time each day to review your notes from that day as well as completing any assignments or readings for the next day should be high on your priority list. Success expert Stephen Covey said, "The key is not to prioritize what is on your schedule, but to schedule your priorities."

iii) SUCCESS FAVOURS THOSE WHO ARE PREPARED

It's been said that the harder you work, the luckier you will get. Another way of saying this is that success comes most often to those who have prepared for it.

Geoff Colvin in his bestselling book *Talent Is Overrated* states, "The factor that explains the most about great performance is something researchers call deliberate practice. Deliberate practice is hard. It hurts. But it works. More of it equals better performance. Tons of it equals great performance."

It might be more fun to do something other than attend all your classes. It might be more fun to do something other than your readings each day. It might be more fun to do something other than preparing study notes each day after class. It might even be more fun to daydream (or text, or surf the internet) than pay attention in class and record lecture notes. But, if you want to be successful in university (or in anything else in life), there are times when hard work is necessary.

Colvin's research goes a step further than just emphasizing hard work. The previous quote from his book talks about something called "deliberate practice". The best athletes or top musicians in the world don't just spend more hours practicing; they spend more hours of deliberate practice. Deliberate practice could be defined as practicing what is most important to be successful.

A professional golfer who wants to be more successful doesn't just spend more hours playing golf each day; he or she spends this time carefully working on a specific aspect of his/her game that will contribute to being more successful. Applying this principle to university success, you will not necessarily be more successful just because you attend all your classes or just because you spend hours each day looking at your texts. To be successful, you need to engage in what is termed "deliberate practice".

Deliberate practice means that when you

are in class, you are fully engaged in the learning by participating whenever possible by answering or even asking questions, by taking careful notes that highlight what is most important, and by preparing before the class to already have some knowledge and other background information related to the lecture. To do this while your friends might be having fun can be hard work. To do this when you are tired (or bored) can be hard work. But this is an example of deliberate practice. This is the type of preparation that leads to success. This is the type of preparation that leads to what some would call "good luck". Thomas Jefferson said, "I'm a great believer in luck, and I find that the harder I work the more I have of it."

Some students spend hours and hours studying, only to fail their exams. In talking with these students, I often discovered that their definition of studying is reading their text or notes over and over again (sometimes even with one eye on the TV, or both ears on their favourite music). While this may approach may be an example of working hard, it is not an example of working smart. Deliberate practice requires you to do the things that will help you to be more successful. It is not just about spending more time. I could go out on a golf course and practice twelve hours a day and never improve my game unless my practice is based on doing the things that will actually make a difference in my game.

Research in the area of studying would tell you that simply reading your notes and text (regardless of how many hours you do this) is not going to help you to be as successful as actually forming questions that might be asked (from noting questions that your professor asks in class or even from old tests that might be stored in the university library) and then writing your answers to these questions (using your notes and text to help you).

Another simple technique is to make "study cards". An easy way to do this is to purchase small file cards. Use a different colour for each of your classes. Each day after class, form a list of questions based on the class lectures (and related text references).

On one side of each file card, write your questions. On the backs of each file card, write your answers. By doing this daily, you will have a complete set of study cards when exam time arrives. You won't need to waste time creating new cards; they will already be done for you. This is an example of studying in a manner that will help to increase your success. This is an example of deliberate practice. Most importantly, this is an example of success favouring those who are prepared.

Some students find it helpful to study in a group with other students. This has the advantage of helping you to look at the course content from different perspectives. The kind of questions you thought might be on the exam might be different than those of another student. Study groups can help you to ensure that you haven't missed any key concepts within the course. They can help to reinforce your learning in a fun way. If you are going to form a study group, challenge yourself to work with the best students you can gather together. It has been said that we become the average of the five people we spend most of our time with; strive to spend your time with other students who want to be successful (and who have a proven record of being successful).

If you believe that your study skills are weak, ask your professor or teaching assistant for help. There are generally on-campus workshops that focus on helping students to improve their study skills.

Being prepared is not just about paying attention in class or engaging in meaningful study; it is also about how you prepare for your classes. You should have a course outline or a syllabus. Your course outline provides you with an overview of the topics you will be studying and it also provides the order in which you will study them (and often has the related dates as well).

Your learning in any class can be tremendously enhanced when you prepare for your classes by reading and even researching related materials for the topic of your next class. To already have some background information about what the professor is going to be teaching can help to increase your learning. In addition, it can help you to contribute in a meaningful way to class discussions and it can also help you to identify any new concepts that you don't understand so that you can ask questions of clarification in class.

Waiting until the night before your exams before trying to clarify anything you don't understand is not going to contribute to being successful.

Another important aspect of being prepared is related to how you organize your time. Throughout this book there are some tips on time management. For now, one of the most important aspects of managing your time (which really means managing yourself) is to have an agenda (whether in a book form or in a digital form on your computer or cell phone) where you record every assignment, every test, and every other commitment that you have in your life. This agenda should include clear notations as to due dates and what is expected for any assignments, projects or tests. Each day after your classes, it is critical that you review your agenda as you decide what you are going to do for your homework. When you have multiple upcoming assignments/tests it is important to prioritize what you have to do, and that you set a schedule that you can follow that will take you step-by-step to completing your work.

Leaving assignments and studying for tests at the last minute can be overwhelming and can result in poor marks (and create stress for you). My experience with university students tells me that a significant number of students fail courses in their first year because they waited until the last minute to complete major assignments or to study for exams. The way you organize yourself can directly contribute to being more successful in university.

iv) UNDERSTAND THE DIFFERENCES BETWEEN HIGH SCHOOL AND UNIVERSITY

When I was a high school guidance counsellor, a common question that students asked me was, "How is university different than high school?" As a university professor, I often heard students say, "This is so different than high school." So how is university different than high school, and how can your understanding of these differences help you to be more successful in university?

For many years, as the Head of various high school guidance departments, I received a print-out of the final marks for all our former students from the various universities they now attended (this rarely happens anymore because of privacy laws). The main reason for receiving the university marks was to help high school teachers better understand how their assessment of students compared to what actually happened in university. The reality was that most first year university students suffered a mark drop, on average, of about 10-15%. In other words, first year university students found that their marks, on average, were 10-15% lower than what they experienced in high school.

There are a few reasons that contribute to this decrease in marks. By understanding these reasons, you have a better chance of maintaining your high school mark average (or even improving it) throughout university.

First of all, one of the major differences between high school and university is that you will now be much more independent. For example, if you live in a campus residence or in some form of student housing, you will now be making your own daily decisions without the influence of your parents. This can include (but is not limited to) what you are going to eat, what time you wake up, what time you go to bed, whether you go to your classes, how you spend your free time, whether you do your homework, and so on. Students who have developed good success habits during high school will often continue these in university, especially if these habits are the result of being self-motivated instead of constantly being "pushed" by a parent or teacher. On the other hand, students with poor work habits and/or who depended on their parents to remind them when assignments were due, etc. may find the sudden independence leading to a lack of success.

In university, much more than high school, you will find that you are in charge of more aspects of your life. If you recognize this, and attempt to make wise decisions for yourself (based on many of the tips and strategies in this book), you can be successful. Not only can you enjoy academic success, but you can also achieve a greater sense of confidence as you establish yourself as a person, independent from your parents.

Another difference between high school and university is your relationship with your teachers. In high school, successful students often establish a close bond with their teachers. Given that high school classes tend to be much smaller in size than university classes, your high school teachers generally knew you by your first name. In addition, as a result of participating on teams and in clubs (where your teachers may be your coaches and/or staff advisors), you often develop strong rapport with your teachers.

For many students, the "bond" that they formed with their high school teachers and the comfort of being in a smaller class contributed strongly to their success. Suddenly in university where classes in your first two years are often over 50 students (and some might even be over 100 students), it is more difficult to establish a bond with a professor. In addition, some students find it much harder in a large class to get involved in discussions (and the reality is that in some very large classes, there may be little discussion).

Having said this, there are still ways you can create a positive relationship with your professors that can make your learning more enjoyable and help you to be more successful.

Professors in university are not likely going to be starting their classes by taking attendance and by trying to learn the names of their students. Therefore, it is your responsibility to find a way to introduce yourself to your professor. Whenever you answer a question in class, remind your professor of your name. Whenever your professor teaches a strong lesson, compliment him or her. If you have questions about an assignment, make an appointment to see your professor in person (be sure to prepare some specific questions so you don't waste the professor's time). As you create a relationship between you and the professor, this will help to make your class more enjoyable and it will also create some rapport between the two of you which could be helpful if you need some individual feedback on what you might do to improve your marks if you ever have this need. Note as well, you can take this same approach with any teaching assistants who are involved with your classes.

Another excellent way to establish a positive relationship with a professor is to apply/ volunteer to assist with any research projects that your professor might be involved with.

A big difference between high school and university relates to your attendance. In many high schools, if you miss a class your parents would receive a telephone call or an email from the school alerting them of your absence. In addition, your teacher would keep a daily record of whether you were in class, or not. There is this constant expectation in high school for you to be attending your classes. This generally changes in university. In many classes, no attendance is even taken. No one is going to chase you (or contact your parents) if you miss any classes. Some students respond to this freedom by missing classes if they have something better to do, or if the class is boring or too hard. It doesn't take too many missed classes before you might find yourself in academic trouble. If you want to be successful in university, it is your responsibility to attend all your classes (and to be there on time).

Another difference between high school and university is the amount of expected work you are required to do out of class. From my experience, most high school students do the homework that has been assigned to them, but tend to do no homework if nothing has been assigned. This changes in university. As a rule of thumb, to be successful in university, you should be doing at least 1-2 hours of work outside of class for every hour you spend in class. And most important, you should be doing this work even if you have not been assigned any homework. As mentioned earlier, successful students review their lessons every day, highlighting important points in their notes, preparing study notes, completing related readings, and preparing for their next class.

Another difference between high school and university is that in high school you generally have the same classes each day. In university, you might only have a class in a certain subject area once a week, and you might even have a day or possibly two where you don't have any classes. Generally, your university classes will be much longer than your high school classes. As a result of what I have said so far, consider the reality that when you miss one university class it is similar to missing a complete week of work in high school. Taking this a step further, if you miss four university classes, this would be similar to missing a month of work in high school. I have seen some university students miss three or four classes, and then wonder why they are struggling to pass. Success in university is often very directly related to attending all your classes.

University success is definitely directly proportional to your own self-discipline as it relates to attendance and completing your work. No one is going to do it for you. The reality is that it is unlikely that anyone is going to give you a "push" if you need it. Success in university, similar to success in your eventual career, comes from being self-motivated. For many students, this is the biggest difference between high school and university. You are completely responsible for your success or your lack of success; the sooner you realize this and take control of your life, the sooner you will experience success at university.

Having more freedom at university can also expose you to decisions that you have to make related to sex, drugs and alcohol. Poor decisions in any of these areas could lead to negative consequences in your personal life as well as impacting your success at university.

There are definitely some differences between high school and university. These differences can be positive or they can be negative depending on your attitude towards them and your level of self-discipline. The development of will-power and self-control will contribute to success throughout your life. Winners develop certain habits; self-discipline is one of them.

Jesse Owens, the four-time Olympic gold medalist, said, "We all have dreams. But in order to make dreams come into reality, it takes an awful lot of determination, dedication, self-discipline, and effort." In becoming successful at university, you would do well to master the traits that Owens identifies.

Here is a list of some other differences between high school and university that I have heard students talk about. University provides:

- greater opportunities to form new friendships with people from around the world

- the opportunity to build stronger friendships with others (after all, you are often with them 24/7)

- the opportunity to take a wider range of courses

- the opportunity to study more in-depth courses in your major area of interest

- the opportunity to become involved in research related to your major interest

- the opportunity to join a wider range of clubs or teams

- the opportunity to learn from experts in your field of studies

- the opportunity to form connections with people from around the world (connections that may be someday very important to you in your career)

- the opportunity to have fun as you get involved in a wide range of activities

- greater opportunities to get involved in volunteer work

- opportunities to work part-time on campus

- greater time off between academic years providing you with the opportunity to gain invaluable work experience or travel

- opportunities to study in other countries

- more opportunities to make your own choices

- exposure to greater learning opportunities

- the opportunity for possible internships in some fields of study

- the opportunity to be more challenged

- the opportunity to become independent

- the necessary requirements for a future career

- the opportunity to complete a Degree

While I have likely forgotten a few things that could have been included in the above list, hopefully I have provided enough thoughts that you can now see that there are many advantages to attending a university. One final huge difference between high school and university that I would like to mention concerns financial matters.

For the most part in high school, most students never have to be concerned about financing their education as public high schools are free for most students in most countries. Although you might have had to pay for some supplies here or there, or for some field trips, for the most part you likely had help from your parents. University is a very different experience in this regard.

Most students (and their parents) are often shocked when they realize how much university will cost. Although there are various forms of government assistance and although your parents may be helping you (but not necessarily), it is still critical to budget your money regardless of where it is coming from.

Some students drop out of school by the end of their first term or semester because they run out of the money that was supposed to last them for the complete school year. Other students, after graduating from university, sometimes have to work in menial jobs, completely unrelated to their area of studies, because they need to begin to pay back their student loans, and they can't afford to wait to find their dream job.

It is often said that money concerns contribute more to personal problems than any other single factor. Similarly, money problems can have a detrimental affect on your success in university. Learning how to manage your money in university is a skill that will be a huge benefit to you for the rest of your life. Although it is not within the scope of this book to provide a detailed overview of how to manage your money (I have written another book titled *Live Debt Free* that might be helpful to you), here are a few tips.

First of all, the key to financial success is spending less than you make. Rewording this for a university student, the key to financial success is spending less than you have (or will have if you are also working part-time as you attend university). To do this, you need to calculate how much money you still have available after you pay for tuition, room/board, books, and other fees. You will then need to divide this amount of money by the number of weeks you will be at university during the school year. The result from this shows you how much you could spend each week in order to avoid running out of money before the school year ends. At the beginning of each week, you need to know exactly how much money you have available to spend, and at the end of each week you need to evaluate how you did. If you spend a little more than you budgeted during some weeks, then the following week, you need to spend a little less. If you are constantly running out of money, you need to either become more self-disciplined in your spending or you could consider getting a part-time job.

So, how is university different than high school? Hopefully the previous few pages have highlighted some of the important differences for you, and the rest are waiting for you to discover.

v) KNOW WHERE TO GET HELP

At some time or another you are going to require some help during your studies. It might be that you need a map to find your classes during your first week of school. It might be that you need some help in choosing your courses. You might need help in purchasing your books. You might also need help to get a locker, a bus pass, information on clubs, information about medical assistance on campus, study skills, and on the list could go.

I will keep this simple. During orientation and your first week or two at university, keep a record of the various services that are available at your university. Enter important campus phone numbers and email addresses into your cell phone.

There are a surprisingly number of staff members available at any university to help you. The key is for you become aware of these services before you actually require them.

vi) HAVE A REASON TO SUCCEED

University is hard work, even when you are in a program that you absolutely love. University might be described as running in a marathon. On average, students spend four years at university completing an undergraduate degree. Four years is a long time, especially when you also consider the number of years you spent in school before arriving at university.

To help you complete your degree, you might find it useful to identify some benefits that you believe you will achieve by graduating from university. I often find that successful students have a very clear vision as to how graduating from university is going to help them. For many, graduating from university provides the qualifications for a job or even for future education. For others, graduating from university provides a sense of pride. For some, graduating from university is the reward for hard work and persistence. For others, graduating from university will open the door for new opportunities. And finally for some, graduating from university is simply a concrete symbol to demonstrate their love of learning.

Whatever reasons you have for graduating from university, it can be helpful for you to write these down. I have worked with some students who created a success poster which showed various pictures of how they believe their life will be after they graduate from university. Whichever technique you use, keep these words or images clearly before you. Whenever you are struggling with the amount of work you have to do or whenever you experience some aspect of failure, look at your list of reasons for wanting to graduate. If you have established a powerful list of ways in which you will benefit by graduating from university, these reasons can help to motivate you to be successful.

Jack Canfield and Mark Victor Hansen, two of the most successful authors during the past few decades, wrote, "The main reason most people struggle professionally and personally is simply a lack of focus." Whatever you are focusing on can play a direct role in your success, or your lack of success, at university.

vii) BELIEVE YOU CAN SUCCEED

Various successful people throughout history have stated something along the lines of: "You can if you believe you can." Of course, the opposite of this is true as well.

To be successful in anything you do in life, you have to believe that you can do it. Unfortunately, some students believe that university is going to be too hard for them, and in some cases give up before they really get going. If you can achieve the requirements to be accepted at a university, for most students it's not a matter of whether you have the ability to be successful; rather it is a matter of whether you have the right attitude (and work habits) to be successful.

It has been said that changing your attitude can change your altitude. To be successful, you must first believe that you will be successful. While this book is packed with tips and strategies to help you to be more successful, in the end these suggestions will matter very little if your mind is telling you that you can't be successful.

What we focus on is who we often become. What we think about the most generally directs our lives. Our mind can be like a steering wheel helping to direct us towards our goals, but it can also be a steering wheel turning us away from our goals. And most important, you are the person controlling the steering wheel.

It has often been said by experts in the field of thinking that most people tend to have far more negative thoughts each day than positive thoughts. For many students, the difference between success and failure is often directly related to their thoughts more than their abilities. Some intellectually gifted students fail to complete university because their thoughts sabotage any chance to be successful. On the other hand, some students with average ability achieve greatly in their university studies because their "I can do it" attitude provided the fuel to succeed.

As you look at the tips in the remainder of this book, I suggest that you find two or three suggestions that you believe could make a positive difference for you. Write these thoughts on a piece of paper and carry them with you. Read them every morning and every night. Once these tips actually become part of your habits, browse through this book once again to see if you can find another suggestion or two that could increase your success even more. If so, once again constantly read these tips and attempt to live by them.

When you develop the appropriate habits of success, you will be successful beyond your dreams.

It is my hope that this book can help you to be a successful university. It is my hope his/her degree, one of the students who has a positive, life-enhancing university experience.

It also my hope that long before you attend the ceremonies to celebrate your graduation that you find happiness and purpose in your life each day.

1. Take 100% responsibility
    for being successful.
    It is not up to anyone else other
    than you to achieve your dreams.

2. Before you attend the university
    campus, spend some time surfing
    the university website. In
    particular look for services that the
    university offers that might be
    beneficial to you.

3. Professors are there to help you.
    They want you to be successful.
    When in doubt, ask for help.

4. Plan on arriving at the university
    so that you can participate in all
    orientation activities.

5. Focus on your successes,
    not your failures.

6. Set a regular time to
    communicate with your family.

7. Compliment at least
    one person every day.

8. Buy software at "educational
    prices". The campus bookstore
    often has the best deals.

9. It takes less time to fix a problem
    before it happens.

10. If you need to talk to a professor
    about an assignment, prepare

some questions before
your appointment.

11. Attend all your classes.

12. Nothing would ever get done if
you had to first overcome every
possible obstacle.

13. Exercise and good eating habits
can help you to be more successful.

14. Buy used texts to save money.

15. Being organized is like exercise.
It's not very effective if
you only do it once in awhile.

16. When you have a goal you will tend to be more successful.

17. Eliminate bad habits; repeat good habits.

18. When you choose your courses, carefully read the course descriptions of all the courses that are available to you.

19. If you have a roommate, establish some basic rules such as a time for lights out, room cleanliness, visitors, etc. Establish some rapport with your roommate by focusing on common interests rather than dwelling on your differences.

20. Choosing your courses can be an opportunity to schedule an appointment with your professors to discuss the course content.

21. Ensure that your course selections are completed by the stated deadlines.

22. When you are listening to another person, don't let your eyes wander.

23. Don't take more courses than you need during your first year. There are no bonus marks or prizes for taking more than you have to.

24. Use different coloured file folders

to organize your course materials.

25. If you have an appointment with a professor or any other staff member, always arrive early.

26. Don't worry about things that are out of your control.

27. To be successful it is important to realize that for every hour you spend in class you should be doing at least 1-2 hours of related work outside of class (which can include assignments, projects, readings, preparing for your next class, and preparing for future tests).

28. Keep your words and thoughts consistent with your goals.

29. Only sign up for an early morning class if you are going to be there 100% of the time.

30. Consider taking something completely different for some of your optional courses.

31. Email is forever.
Be careful what you say.

32. Most successful students take accurate notes in class.

33. Choose your courses carefully.

34. Be careful that yesterday doesn't use up too much of today.

35. Before your first day of classes, walk to each of the buildings and locate your actual classrooms so that you will not be late on your first day of classes because you got lost.

36. Your chosen major should be based on both your interests and your abilities. In addition, match your major, if possible, to your eventual career field.

37. Doing well on an assignment is based on the end result, not how many hours it took you to complete it.

38. When you say "please",
be sincere.

39. Don't keep your notes as loose
papers . Either file them in a folder
or keep them in a binder.

40. If you are contacting your
professor by email, this is not the
time to punctuate your email
with cute emoticons and smileys.

41. When you are choosing your
courses you might find it helpful to
go to the university bookstore and
peruse the required texts for any
courses you are considering taking.

42. Whenever you have the

opportunity, talk to senior
students about courses you are
thinking about taking, but in the
end remember you are
responsible for your choices.

43. Faster is not always better.

44. Place your name on
everything you own.

45. Spend most of your time with
successful people.

46. Respect the privacy of others by
using your earphones.

47. The application of what you are

learning is more important
than your ability to memorize
what you have learned.

48. Set a weekly budget and spend
less each day than you intended.

49. The smallest step forward brings
you closer to achieving your goals.

50. Locate your library before you
begin your first day of classes.

51. Talk to other students about
timesaving apps and also
apps to help you be more
organized (such as iStudiezPro,
PocketList, EverNote, and Chegg).

52. If you find yourself constantly losing things, this is a warning that you need to find a way to better organize yourself.

53. Working smarter is more important than working longer.

54. Get a good night's sleep.

55. If you have a concern about a mark in a class, consult with your professor in private, not during your class.

56. Being organized can help to reduce your level of stress.

57. Save money by skyping or texting
your friends and parents
back home instead of calling them.

58. Keep changing your actions until
you get the desired results.

59. Judging others usually takes up
more of your time
than accepting them.

60. Consider e-books to save money.

61. Never plagiarize.

62. The most successful students are
those who work consistently every
day, rather than waiting until the

night before an assignment is due or the night before a test before they start to work.

63. Discover what services exist at your school such as recreational, tutoring, and various help labs.

64. The only appropriate excuse is that there are no excuses.

65. Locate any cafeterias and all campus restaurants before the first day of school. If you have a meal plan, ensure that you understand where you can eat and how often.

66. If you miss a class, find out what

you missed from other people in the class. Don't waste a professor's time because you missed a class.

67. It might make sense to find out what your computer needs are going to be before you rush out and buy one the week before school begins.

68. There is always a cost: understand the demands of your time before you say yes to any requests.

69. When you choose your courses, have a backup plan.

70. After 2 or 3 classes, if the course

is completely different than what
you were expecting, or the
professor's teaching style is alien to
you, consider changing this
course to one in your backup plan.

71. If you want to get a higher mark,
it is best to say, "What can I do to
improve my mark?" instead of
saying, "I need a higher mark."
Show the professor that you are
willing to work harder to earn
a higher mark.

72. Treat others the way
you want to be treated.

73. Locate on-campus and
off-campus convenience stores.

74. Lack of direction is often the real reason for a lack of time.

75. A strategy without a commitment is not a strategy.

76. Use abbreviations and symbols in your notes to save time.

77. If you are on a waitlist for a class, keep checking to see if an opening has occurred. By the end of the first week of classes, there may be some students who were ahead of you on the waitlist who are no longer interested in the course.

78. Have a firm handshake.

79. First impressions are important.

80. The first step in achieving any goal is to write it down.

81. Perform one random act of kindness each day.

82. Limits are what you accept in your mind.

83. Thank your professors for their feedback. Learn from any criticism you receive.

84. If you need to drop a course, ensure that you do it before the stated deadlines; otherwise

you might end up paying
for the complete course.

85. If you are going in the wrong
direction, going faster still
won't help you.

86. When selecting your courses
consider the time requirements
that work best for you. Would you
be more successful if you had
one or two classes every day
or would you be more
successful if most of your classes
were scheduled on two or three days
leaving you with some
free days to complete your
assignments (and/or possibly
work at a part-time job)?

87. Before you begin any project, ensure that you have all the required materials.

88. If you have the opportunity, work as a research assistant for any professors who are teaching in an area you would like to major in.

89. The most flexible trees survive the greatest storms.

90. If a personal problem is making it difficult for you to be successful at university, make an appointment to see a counsellor on your campus.

91. Sometimes opportunity comes

dressed in work clothes.

92. Ensure that you have the
necessary prerequisites
for any courses that you choose.

93. Being busy and being productive
are not necessarily the same thing.

94. Before you venture out on the
campus at night, be aware of
volunteers or possible security
staff members who can accompany
you to ensure your safety.

95. Use a prepaid debit card
instead of a credit card.

96. Choose a major that builds on both your interests and abilities.

97. Turn off your cell phone during your classes.

98. Ensure that you understand which courses are compulsory for your program.

99. Accept that everyone makes mistakes.

100. If you do poorly on your first few assignments, don't get discouraged. Talk to your professor about how you can improve. If necessary, talk to someone on staff who helps with

student success.

101. If you don't understand something, ask for help.

102. If you have a financial need, make an appointment to see an advisor in the Financial Aid Office. There are often various forms of financial help for students with need.

103. Avoid too much sun (and don't forget to use sunscreen when you are in the sun). Staying healthy can help you to stay successful.

104. If possible, schedule your

classes for the time of day
when you know you are at your best
and when you know you will attend
100% of your classes.

105. Unless you have a better way
of doing it, don't criticize the
suggestion you have been given.

106. If you are in a large class,
attend all small group discussions
related to the class.

107. Surprise a friend with
a little unexpected gift.

108. There are times when it is
necessary to move on to the next
question even when you haven't

finished the question before it.

109. If it has to be done, then do it.

110. The secret of being successful is knowing what you want to achieve.

111. When your professor hands you a course outline (or syllabus) on your first day of class, keep this information in a safe place. It may include thoughts on how to be successful in this class as well as the professor's policies on attendance, lateness, and penalties for handing in late assignments. This information is critical to your success in any course. Read the information often, and highlight the important points. The handout

will also likely include your course reading material. Even though a professor might not tell you what you should be reading each week, it is your responsibility to sort this out and do any readings that are related to the current topic that your professor is teaching.

112. You will be more successful if you do your homework each day rather than leaving it until the weekend to complete it in a marathon session.

113. Whenever you find success, keep repeating whatever you are doing.

114. Don't blame others when

things go wrong.

115. Conflicts are better resolved in private than they are in public.

116. If everything is falling apart, talk to an advisor about reducing your course load. It is generally better to complete a few of your courses then to throw them all away. In some courses you might even be able to negotiate an "incomplete" and then finish your course work over the summer.

117. Before you begin any task always understand what it is that you are really trying to do.

118. Instead of looking for excuses, look for ways to be successful.

119. Waking up 15 minutes earlier each day might help you to have a more relaxing and productive day.

120. Look for opportunities.

121. You will be more successful in completing large assignments if you develop a plan and do a little each day on them.

122. Clearly identify the problem before you attempt to find some solutions.

123. There may be times when no homework has been assigned. When this happens, give yourself some homework.

124. Make a financial plan. Some students drop out of university because they run out of money. Budget wisely.

125. If you need more money, consider working part-time.

126. Be optimistic.

127. When you are given an assignment, ensure that you understand exactly what you are to do before you begin.

If you have any confusion, talk to your professor or his/her teaching assistant. Waiting until the last minute to complete an assignment could cause real problems for you if there is something you don't understand and you are unable to reach your professor for help.

128. Research scholarships and in-course awards that might be available.

129. A great assignment often requires several drafts. You can't complete several drafts if you wait until the last minute to complete the assignment.

130. Identify someone who is

successful in the way that you want to be successful and then imitate whatever they do.

131. Focus on what is most important.

132. Whatever it is that you have to do, do it now.

133. Other people should never be the victim of your jokes.

134. You are in charge of your grades.

135. Make a list of reasons why you want to succeed.

136. Understand who the people are who are most important to you and keep in contact with them.

137. When you study, you will be more successful if you focus on one subject area for several hours rather than changing subjects every 10-15 minutes.

138. In completing any task the single most important word to remember is "action".

139. The best way to handle "test stress" is to be overly prepared.

140. Keep a song in your head that makes you happy.

141. We can't change what happened yesterday, but we can change what will happen tomorrow.

142. Anger generally hurts you more than it hurts others.

143. Choose your courses in a manner that provides a comfortable workload balance.

144. Go for a walk.

145. Find a reason to talk to your professor one-to-one so that he/she knows who you are and also knows that you are serious about learning (and you are

interested in the content
of this class).

146. Plan your studying for an exam
so that you get a good night's sleep
before the exam.

147. Live beneath your means.

148. Get involved in activities that
are offered on your campus.

149. Instead of thinking about what
you have to do next, focus on what
you are doing right now.

150. When you wake up in the
morning, state 3 things

you are looking forward to today.

151. Successful people build on their strengths.

152. Professors often provide hints or clues as to what is going to be on an exam. Listen carefully throughout the course for any topics that are emphasized.

153. Be a good listener. Your ears will not get you into the same trouble as your mouth might.

154. Studying is about how much you learn, rather than how many hours you study. Learn study techniques that can help you to be more

successful. These could include
learning to highlight important
parts of your notes. These could
also include using practice
tests (you can even make your
own with friends) and writing out
the answers. The worst way to study
is to simply read your notes and
texts. Effective studying requires
you to write and/or state
your learning in response
to sample questions.

155. Accept change.

156. Generally the same old ways
achieve the same old results.

157. Clubs that you join can help you
to meet new friends. They can also

help you to establish contacts which
might someday be beneficial to you
as you seek employment
after graduating from university.

158. If you find yourself getting
overwhelmed, there is a
counselling department on campus
that can direct you to someone
who can help you to be
better organized and deal
more positively with stress.

159. Sometimes in order to see
things differently, you need to try a
different pair of glasses.

160. When you are studying,
turn off your cell phone.

161. Some people study better listening to music; others don't. It is important to understand what works best for you.

162. Before you fall to sleep at night, state 3 things you are thankful for.

163. Let others help you.

164. If you fail a course, consider taking a summer course to keep you on schedule for graduating when you were expecting to graduate.

165. Be a positive talker.

166. If you are uncomfortable with any form of orientation activity at the university (or as a part of joining a team or club), then don't do it.

167. Invest in some earphones that also have a noise-cancelling feature. Sometimes you may need to listen to silence in order to concentrate on your homework.

168. Along with well-organized notes, keep all tests (with correct answers). These materials can form the foundation of your study resources for your exams.

169. At the beginning of each day,

identify what you want to
accomplish during the day.

170. Discuss your course
requirements with an advisor.
When selecting your courses,
ensure that you are taking any
compulsory courses that you
require for graduation
in your program.

171. Students don't generally plan
to fail; sometimes they
just fail to plan.

172. Finding the best in others will
help them to find the best in you.

173. Practice is integral to success

provided that you are
practicing correctly.

174. If you have to complete a group project, choose the best people you can find to be your partners.

175. Be the change you would like to see around you.

176. Watch your drinks at any social gatherings, and never get drunk.

177. Successful people are persistent.

178. When you receive a test or assignment back from your professor, ensure that you know the

correct answers or what you could
have done to achieve
a better mark.

179. Pace yourself.

180. Network with people who
share your interests, whether
these are staff members
or other students.

181. Schedule your most important
tasks for the time of the day when
you know you are the
most productive.

182. Treat the environment as
though it is one
of your best friends.

183. Although study groups can be very helpful to you, it is still important to also study on your own.

184. Eating well can increase success in all areas of your life.

185. Choose your friends wisely. What they do and say can also affect your reputation.

186. There is a tendency to become the average of the people you spend most of your time with.

187. Let others finish what they have to say before you respond.

188. Generally, it takes less time to do a job today then it does to postpone it until tomorrow.

189. Always be early for class.

190. Read to understand, not just to memorize.

191. Even the largest mountain can be scaled one step at a time.

192. Always back up your computer files.

193. Be as self-starter.

194. Think big goals;
enjoy small accomplishments.

195. If you can no longer afford your
monthly credit card payments, then
stop using your credit card.

196. Verifying the details of
anything you have to do can be
a timesaver and help you to be
more successful.

197. Avoid "ifs" and "buts".

198. At times, school can be stressful.
Understand which strategies and
techniques work best for you
in dealing with stress.

199. Long term goals should have a step you can work on each day.

200. Smile.

201. If you don't like what you see in your future; create a new one.

202. If you are struggling in a class, there may be remedial help, extra seminars, and tutoring possibilities to help you.

203. Never cheat.

204. During a lecture you should constantly be taking notes, although it is also important to

participate. Strong notes are often
the key to being successful
in preparing for exams.

205. Sometimes opportunity blows
quietly in the wind.
Learn to listen.

206. If you are commuting to school,
practice travelling to classes before
school begins so you know how
much time you need to be on time.

207. Success rarely happens
overnight.

208. Thank others when
they compliment you.

209. Inflexible goals are often best achieved by a flexible process.

210. Respect the privacy of others.

211. If you are given any readings before a class, do them. This will increase your learning during the lecture.

212. Eat a slow, nutritious breakfast.

213. There are likely people, such as your parents, who may have played a significant role in helping you to reach university; don't forget about them now that you are living apart from them.

214. Learn to ignore your negative
thoughts in the same way you
might ignore someone who
is pestering you.

215. Every once in awhile,
push yourself beyond
your comfort zone.

216. The main job is always to
keep the main job the main job.

217. Introduce yourself to
your professors.

218. When you answer a question
in class, remind everyone
of your name until your
professor calls you by your name.

219. Enter any emergency call numbers for your university campus into your cell phone.

220. If you are working hard but not getting very good results, you might need to change the way you are working.

221. As you take notes during the class, ensure that you record your professor's view on the topic as your prime focus.

222. Accept others as they are, not as you want them to be.

223. When you are upset at someone, go for a walk before

you talk to them.

224. Pack things away in a manner
that makes it easier to
unpack them for use.

225. Less is often more.

226. Review your class notes each
day after class. Highlight anything
you think could be important.
You could even begin to write
study cards or form a list of
questions that you think might
appear on an exam.

227. Place a paper towel in the
bottom of any container
you use to hold pens.

228. On a test, always answer the questions you are asked.

229. Join a club.

230. The key points in any lecture often occur at the beginning of a lecture and in the summary at the end. Don't be late for class and don't be in a rush to leave as class is ending.

231. Taking a day to rest when you are beginning to feel sick may be better than trying to attend all your classes and then missing a week because you get really sick.

232. Get involved in special events.

233. You can't please everyone
all the time.

234. There's a time to work
and a time to play;
strive for a balance in your life.

235. Have a friend in each of your
classes who can tell you what you
missed if you are ever sick,
and do the same for them as well.

236. If you are making a
presentation in class,
don't read from your visuals.
Relevant pictures with one or two
words that relate to what the

picture represents are far more
effective than presenting a
PowerPoint (or similar program)
where you simply read
what's on each slide.

237. Some see possibilities where
others see problems.

238. If there are any extra seminars,
assignments, or rewriting tests
you can do to achieve additional
marks, do them.

239. Sometimes what you think
you have to do is
more tiring than what you
actually have to do.

240. School is demanding; don't make it more difficult by using/ abusing drugs and alcohol.

241. Form a study group to ask each other questions.

242. Forgive yourself, and move on.

243. Join a team.

244. Have others proof your work before you hand it in.

245. Whenever you have a presentation to make, practice the presentation in front of someone else who can time you and

provide some feedback.

246. Develop the habit of praising yourself even when others don't.

247. Ensure you always know what is required on any assignment.

248. Work smarter instead of harder.

249. The main thing should always be the main thing.

250. If an email upsets you, wait for a day before responding to it.

251. Avoid negative people.

252. You will never know
if you don't try.

253. People who are always trying
to please others rarely
please themselves.

254. Don't make the same
mistake twice.

255. It's okay to be happy.

256. Failure can be a stepping stone
to success.

257. Prioritize what you have to do
and start with your
most important tasks.

258. If you are making a class
presentation, arrive early
to ensure that your audio
visual equipment is working.

259. Sometimes in order to be more
successful, you will have to change
how you are doing things.

260. Talk to the person who is
most likely to make things
happen for you.

261. Serious problems
require serious help.
There are counsellors on
campus who can assist you.

262. In every setback,

look for a new opportunity.

263. Be curious.

264. Doing it the way you've always
done it may no longer be
the right way to do it.

265. Be enthusiastic.

266. If you love what you are doing,
it will be easier to be successful.

267. Have a written list of things
you have to complete each day
and review the list often.

268. Avoid junk food and drinks with a high sugar content.

269. Have a specific place where you always put those "little things" like your keys, wallet/purse, etc.

270. Relax.

271. Remember that a strong finish is as important as a good start.

272. If your desk is generally covered with small notes to yourself, try keeping one master "To Do" list instead.

273. Always write your ideas down

before you forget them.

274. The key to an effective
presentation is to talk,
not read. Stories and concrete
materials can enhance your
presentation and help
you to feel more comfortable.

275. Learn from the past
and plan for the future,
but live in the present.

276. In all things, be yourself.

277. Keep eliminating what doesn't
work until you find what does.

278. Focus on what's right, rather than what's wrong.

279. Always do the right thing.

280. If you have to take a compulsory course that is not a strength for you ensure that you are taking the easiest level that is permitted.

281. The first step is always just that.

282. Praise others in public; resolve conflicts in private.

283. If you can't change what you would like to change, maybe

you need to change your
attitude towards it.

284. You have to know what you
want before you can get it.

285. Obstacles often occur in
proportion to the number
of times you take your eyes
off your goals.

286. Action is the key to success.

287. Place time limits on any task
you are working on.

288. Offer to teach some
other students.

289. A few minutes at the end of each day organizing yourself for tomorrow will usually take less time than if you save the same task for the morning.

290. Sometimes in order to have a friend, you must first be one.

291. Drink lots of water.

292. Take one minute mental vacations.

293. Avoid loaning money to friends because you might end up with neither.

294. Solve your own problems before you try to rescue everyone else.

295. Live the life you imagine.

296. If you are taking an online course, keep in mind that the professor can access how many times you have logged into the course, how much of the course content you are reading, and how many times you reply to others or to the professor. If you rarely log into your course and rarely get involved in any discussions this information will be available to your professor as he evaluates your work in the course.

297. Spend most of your time with those who bring out the

best in you.

298. Don't gamble.

299. You don't have to stay up at
night to be successful;
you just have to stay awake
during the day.

300. What will your life look like
5 years from now? What can you
do today to take one step
towards making this happen?

301. If you have the same problem
today as you had last week,
perhaps it's time to find a new
approach for solving it.

302. Reward yourself for working hard.

303. Leave everything a little better than you found it.

304. If English is not your first language, ensure that you are aware of all forms of assistance that are available to help you achieve greater fluency in English.

305. Try to see things from the viewpoint of other people.

306. Set a specific time to do your homework.

307. Keep up on your readings
each day.

308. While you should attempt
to attend all your classes, this is
even more critical in the week
before your exams when professors
may review what is important
or drop some hints as to key areas
that you should be studying.

309. Prepare study notes throughout
your course instead of waiting
until exam time.

310. Write a list of reasons
why graduating from
university will help you.

311. Best friends bring
out the best in you.

312. Sometimes in order to begin to
heal, we have to accept our pain.

313. If the teaching assistants for any
of your classes provide review
sessions leading up to your exams,
then attend all the sessions and
carefully listen for what they
consider to be important.

314. Understand any problem
completely before attempting
to find a solution.

315. Life may not always be fair,
but you can be.

316. Plan on getting at least 8 hours
of sleep the night before
any of your exams.

317. Learning how to type faster
might help you to achieve
more in less time.

318. When tempted to criticize
others, look first at yourself.

319. Expect the best to get the best.

320. Don't say "yes"
when you really mean "no".

321. Learn to disagree
without being disagreeable.

322. Winning is the result of developing certain habits; unfortunately so is losing.

323. Professors tend to ask exam questions about the things they talk about the most.

324. Strive to be more in control of yourself and less in control of others.

325. Watch the sun rise.

326. The library may have archives of old exams in your course that you can use to practice.

327. Use the words *"next time"* instead of *"if only"*.

328. Fill your head with positive thoughts.

329. Deadlines are usually less threatening after you have taken the first step in reaching them.

330. When you write an exam, plan your time so that you don't end up spending too much time on one question which could result in you not completing the exam.

331. Accept that everyone has bad days.

332. Remember that a dream without action is still just a dream.

333. Constantly imagine being successful, and constantly work towards making this happy.

334. Don't be so busy looking at a door that has closed on you that you fail to see the one that is now opening.

335. On multiple-choice tests, eliminate the wrong answers before you decide on the correct one.

336. Good luck is often the result of good preparation.

337. Treat everyone as an equal.

338. If you want to change your life, begin by changing your attitude.

339. Set aside a specific time each day to read and reply to your messages.

340. It is your life; own your decisions.

341. Pay attention to the details.

342. The most important thing about goals is having one.

343. Form a clear picture of what you want to achieve.

344. On any test, answer the question that has been asked. You won't help yourself if you go in an entirely different direction in an attempt to show how much you have learned. As you write your answer constantly reread the question to ensure that you are answering it.

345. Focus on one task at a time.

346. There are times when handing an assignment in on time, even though it is not perfect, is better than trying to make it perfect and handing it in late.

347. Sit near the front of your class.

348. Whenever you are answering a
question, support your thoughts
with quotes and references
from your texts and class notes.
Being specific creates a stronger
answer than being general.

349. A great project is often the
result of many drafts
along the way.

350. Never text or surf the internet
during a class.

351. Our choices are our
responsibility.

352. If you don't do as well as you were expecting on an assignment, ask your professor how you could do better next time.

353. Don't procrastinate.

354. Carefully number your answers on a test and ensure that your name is on every page.

355. Understand before you react.

356. Do more than what is expected.

357. Of all the terrible things that you think might happen, only a few might ever really occur, and

sometimes none of them.

358. There are no bonus marks
for being the first person to finish an
exam. Stay to the end and
reread every question and
proof all your answers.

359. If you know someone who is
successful, copy their good habits.

360. Always keep sight of the bigger
picture while being content with
smaller achievements.

361. Laugh often; but not at the
expense of someone else.

362. Do it right the first time.

363. If you disagree with your grade
on any assignment or exam,
discuss your concerns with your
professor, but do this in private,
rather than in class.

364. You will generally be more
productive if you keep your
schedule somewhere else
than in your head.

365. Set weekly goals.

366. Record all upcoming
assignments and tests
on a calendar that you
look at every day.

367. When you face a huge problem, find some part of it that you can take control of.

368. When faced with large projects, find a way to break the project into small manageable steps. Then establish a timeline for completing each step.

369. Lighten up yourself and you will lighten up your load.

370. Always have others proof your essays. Don't depend on "spell check" and/or "grammar check" to find all your errors.

371. Keep in mind that sometimes

hidden behind big problems
are big opportunities.

372. If you really enjoy a class,
tell your professor, but be sincere.
Don't just do this to try to gain
favour with your professor.

373. Use your library's online
database (or programs like Google
Scholar –www.scholar.google.com)
to find articles and texts that you can
use to complete a course
assignment. In addition, you might
find resources such as WorldCat
(www.worldcat.org)
helpful in providing resources from
other libraries.

374. Keep in contact with those

that you love.

375. If your professor (or teacher assistant) goes out of his/her way to help you with an assignment or some other question you might have had, send them a thank you note to express your gratitude.

376. If you find yourself looking for the same thing today that you lost yesterday, then organize yourself in a way that you will never lose it again.

377. Give others the benefit of the doubt.

378. It is generally better to start your most difficult task first.

379. Let your professor know that you are interested and that you want to learn. You can do this by sitting near the front of your class, ensuring the professor knows your name, and by asking questions and participating in discussions. Professors enjoy teaching students who can actually demonstrate that they have read the materials that were assigned for class.

380. Emphasize quality, not quantity.

381. If possible, volunteer in the department of your subject major.

382. Multi-tasking can lower your level of achievement.

383. It's easier to increase your speed when you know exactly where you are going.

384. Keep a master list of everything you have to do.

385. Use some system to prioritize which items are most important to do today. As you complete each item, cross it off your list with a bold stroke.

386. It takes less time to do it right the first time than to do it over.

387. An unrealistic goal generally
results in a realistic failure.

388. Ask an expert.

389. If you find an article related to
your current topic in a class,
share it with your professor.

390. If you don't know where you're
going, you may end up
somewhere else.

391. Treat everyone you meet
the way you want to be treated.

392. Don't waste your time
learning the "tricks of the trade";

instead, learn the trade.

393. Admit when you are wrong.

394. One of the most respected
personal traits in others is honesty.
To most people, honesty
simply means that you do
what you say you are going to do.

395. Strive for excellence.

396. Think big thoughts,
but enjoy small pleasures.

397. Don't let your possessions
possess you.

398. Never take action
when you are angry.

399. Remember that everyone
loves to feel appreciated.

400. Going to class and
being involved in the class are
two different things; the latter
leads to greater success.

401. Pursue your passion.

NOTES

NOTES

NOTES

Other Books by Brian Harris

CHOOSING
YOUR CAREER

Brian Harris, B.A., M.Ed.

**A Self-Directed Guide to Help You Identify
Your Interests, Abilities and Values to Help You
Choose the Career That is Best for You**

JOBS

**A Practical Manual with a
Free Career Aptitude Test and . . .**

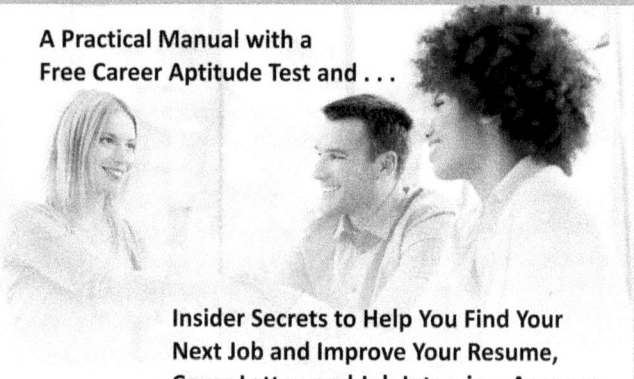

Insider Secrets to Help You Find Your
Next Job and Improve Your Resume,
Cover Letter, and Job Interview Answers
to Help You Get Hired!

Brian Harris, B.A., M.Ed.

Other Books by Brian Harris

LIVE
DEBT FREE

7 Proven Strategies To Help You
Get Rich Without Having
To Change Your Job

Brian Harris, B.A., M.Ed.

TIME MANAGEMENT

Including 471 Tips To Help You Have More Time For Yourself

Brian Harris, B.A., M.Ed.

About the Author

Brian Harris is an award-winning teacher/counselor and best-selling author. He has extensive experience in assisting people with their career planning as well as helping students and adults to find life success. He has also achieved the designation of International Professional Speaker.

Brian lives in Burlington, Canada, with his wife and two teenage daughters. In addition to writing, Brian is a part-time lecturer in counseling at Queen's University. He is also an accomplished artist (www.bcharris.com).

Brian enjoys family trips and is an avid canoeist and scuba diver.

Additional information about Brian can be found at

www.cgscommunications.com